TAKE Off
the
Mask

Take off the Mask
Copyright © 2003 by Teri L. Washington

Requests for information should be addressed to:
Third Dimension Publishing
PO Box 38
Monmouth Junction, NJ 08852
http://www.3ddimension.com

All rights reserved. No part of this book may be reproduced, stored in a retrieval system, or transmitted in any form or by any means – electronic, mechanical, photocopy, recording, or otherwise-without prior written permission of the copyright owner, except by a reviewer who wishes to quote brief passages in connection with a review for inclusion in a magazine, newspaper, or broadcast.

Unless otherwise indicated, all Scripture quotations are taken from The Holy Bible, King James Version. Scripture quotations marked (Amp) are from the Amplified Version of the King James Bible.

ISBN 0-9746567-0-4

TAKE Off *the* Mask

"The Act is Over"

TERI WASHINGTON

Foreword by

Mary Searight

Table of Contents

Dedication
Acknowledgements
Foreword
Preface
Introduction

1. Learned Behavior

2. The Cost of Being Uncovered

3. The Mask of Depression

4. The Mask Revealed

5. The Masquerade

6. Master of Disguise

7. Masked in the Pulpit

8. The Mask of Sickness

9. Unmask Your Need

10. Naked and not Ashamed

11. Covered by the Blood

12. Trust God

13. Take off the Mask

Dedication

Mommy,

I dedicate this book to you, a woman of honor, grace, faith, and determination. Your book is next.

Acknowledgements

To Jehovah Jireh, the God that provides what man cannot. You are my everything. I thank You for purpose, promise, and access to the kingdom.

George, my husband, my hero, my lover, my friend. Thanks for your commitment to love me, your covenant to cherish me, and your determination to hold on to the promise. I love you.

I am so blessed to have children who pray for me. Jazz, you are my life's delight. I am so proud to have a daughter that everybody wants for their own. Blair, my only son in the whole wide world…thanks for the laughter that has been my medicine and your constant reminder that "it's only a test." Destiny, the sunshine of my day, thanks for reminding me to look for God in the little things, like flowers, rainbows and strawberries.

Mommy, for your legacy of faith. Because of you, I am fully persuaded that there is nothing too hard for God.

Daddy, thank you for the anointing that can only come from the Father. I honor you and am proud you call me daughter.

To my Pastors who knew that my latter would be greater than my former. I am forever grateful to God for the covenant connection.

To Debra, Dwight, Neak, Cassandra, Mike, Denitra, and the gang. Thanks for being there, for being close enough to hear me call yet far enough to allow me room to spread my wings. I love you all.

And to all the angels that fed me along the way, thank you. God remembers your labor of love.

Foreword

Mary Searight

Why do we hide from God? Did God not say that what was done in the dark will be brought to the light? At an early age, Teri Washington learned wrongly to value the weight of being hidden, thus lived with the unwillingness and knowledge to become naked before God. It was not long before Teri found herself dying behind a mask of deception.

After walking through what seemed like an endless wilderness, faith spawned and liberation was born. Teri permitted herself to trust God. This engagement catapulted her into the kind of transformation only a renewed mind could bring. Her life is a testimony of the works of Christ. Just as Jesus came to destroy the works of the enemy and then literally ripped the veil from top to bottom, this new author, Teri Washington, has done this and more. She has traced every encounter of her life, thus exposing the enemy. Teri has taken off the mask and is sharing the gift of freedom, for the Son has indeed set her free.

As you read this book, you will be enlightened, enriched, and inspired by the bold leap into what we revere as taboo conversation. My prayer is that you will be renewed in your mind, refreshed in your spirit, and fully persuaded that nothing shall be able to separate you from the love of God which is in Christ Jesus our Lord.

> Your Spiritual Mother,
>
> Co-Pastor, Mary Searight

Preface

I was lying in bed one day when the Lord questioned, "Do you trust Me?" "Lord?" I replied. "Of course, I trust You. What kind of question is that? I've been saved since I was 13 years old. I have been faithful in church and ministry. I have served You, and You ask if I trust You?" Again He asked, "Do you trust Me?"

I have walked with the Lord long enough to know that when He asks a question, He is not asking because He does not know, He is asking so that *I* would know. Over the next several years, God began to show me that I did not trust Him as I thought I did. One year I had to trust Him to be my healer after I was diagnosed with lupus, systemic anemia, and severe mitral valve regurgitation, all at the same time. Another year I had to trust Him to be my guide when He picked me out of my comfort zone and moved me to a strange land among strange people. Then, I had to trust Him to be God when nothing made sense to me. I had to believe that He would never forsake me and that whatever He promised me would come to pass. Had I known the things I would have to endure to have God's promises, I would have declined the invitation to follow Him. But it was too late; I had already given my life to God. I knew that God was bigger than where I was. I knew He was bigger than the God we fit into our little boxes. There was a depth that I wanted to obtain. There was a mystery that I wanted to know about. So I developed a thirst for God. I wanted all that God was and all that He wanted me to be.

Now, I will not say that I kept the faith and completed my course with flying colors. I fussed and complained. Through my process, I found out that I did not trust God or the plan that He had for my life. I wanted to know what God was up to and what He was planning to do with me. I did not want to relinquish control of my life to Him. I also discovered that I had been hiding behind a mask for years, maintaining a façade that was ultimately shutting God out of my life—a disguise that almost killed me.

I will take you through my journey to unmasking. As you read my experience, may you be compelled to remove whatever pretenses you may be hiding behind and discover Jesus loves you just the way you are.

Introduction

The church has historically been a place of refuge. In Ancient Rome, the Catholic Church was the place a person would escape from the judgment of persecutors. The guilty would run into the church and declare "Sanctuary," which meant that as long as they found shelter within the walls of the cathedral no harm would come to them.

Today, these persecutors have entered the church. So when sinners run in expecting a safe haven and find their accusers sitting in the same pews, they camouflage themselves so the accusers won't discover them. The sinner starts behaving like those around him so that he can fit in and go unnoticed.

He takes on the posture of his Elders and those in leadership. Looking for something better, he has come to the House of the Lord, the Citadel, the Fortress, the place of safety. He has learned from a young age that this is the place that he is to come when all else fails. So he comes, but unfortunately, even those who are teaching him are masked. They too have never come to the place where they trust God wholeheartedly. They do not know how to be naked before Him so that all their failures and imperfections are bare at His feet.

It is not the will of God for anyone of us to hide ourselves. Instead, we are instructed to,

"….come boldly to the throne of grace that we may obtain mercy and find grace to help in time of need" (Heb 4:16).

The Amplified version reads,

"…that we may receive mercy (for our failures) when we need it."

In order to have true deliverance in our churches, we must create an atmosphere where it is safe to come with failures.

When you hide behind a mask, you are in acquiescence with the devil and are, therefore, saying that the blood of Jesus is not sufficient to cover your sin. When you continue to hide, you lose all the benefits of Calvary. Jesus cannot protect you, He cannot cover you, He cannot wash you, and your sins cannot be forgiven. However, when you take off the mask and stop the pretenses, the blood of Jesus will cover every indiscretion, and you would be justified by the kingdom of God.

There is a prophetic word being released in the earth. This end time word comes to expose the enemy and to release deliverance to the Body of Christ. God spoke this word to me while I was struggling to breathe behind my own mask. He told me that I could not be fully delivered until I was willing to be naked before Him.

People of God, once we were a nation that was covered, but now the hedge has been lifted because our nation has rejected God. We have rejected Him in our schools, homes, and churches. We have turned our backs on Him and have decided to emulate the world, thus becoming seekers of the flesh. Then, we have disguised ourselves to perpetrate holiness. But I hear God saying, "Since you have rejected Me I will reject you. Since you don't want to represent Me, I will not represent you.

Since you are embarrassed of Me, I will be embarrassed of you. If you don't want to declare that I am your God, then I won't declare that you are My people." God is saying that He is no longer obligated to protect you. There are many who are pretending in the church and hiding behind failures. They are faking it, not just with things or possessions but also with holiness. Not just with images of success but with a form of godliness. God said that some have worn masks for so long that they are afraid to remove them. They fear that the cost of truth will be too great, so they choose to stay covered. Then, the unsaved enter the church and learn from the masked. God said this has been going on for too long, and it must stop. We must dare to remove our masks and let the blood of Jesus cover us.

My pastor, Bishop George C. Searight preached a message entitled "The Last Days." He warned that in the last days there would be a shaking in the heavens and earth. Old Testament prophet Haggai confirms,

> ***"For thus saith the Lord of hosts; Yet once, it is a little while, and I will shake the heavens, and the earth, and the sea, and the dry land" (2:6).***

People are already experiencing a shaking in every area of their lives: finances, health, family, and marriage. The fibers of our morals have been broken down, and things are out of place. Our homes are out of order. Fathers are not in their right places as head of the family. Our children are out of place; they are disobedient and ungrateful. Our teenagers are inhumane and have no regard for themselves and anything else. We adults aren't any better. We are troublemakers, false accusers, backbiters, traitors, and inflated with self-conceit. This is the precursor to a shakedown.

Many years ago, Apostle Paul warned of the onset of this era. He wrote to Timothy:

> *"...in the last days perilous times shall come. For people will be lovers of self and utterly self-centered, lovers of money and aroused by an inordinate greedy desire for wealth, proud and arrogant and contemptuous boasters. They will be abusive, blasphemous, disobedient to parents, ungrateful, unholy and profane. They will be without natural human affection, callous and inhuman, relentless, admitting of no truce or appeasement; they will be slanderers, false accusers, troublemakers, intemperate and loose in*

morals and conduct, uncontrolled and fierce, haters of good. They will be treacherous betrayers, rash, and inflated with self-conceit. They will be lovers of sensual pleasures and vain amusements more than and rather than lovers of God. For although they hold a form of piety true religion, they deny and reject and are strangers to the power of it. Their conduct belies the genuineness of their profession. Avoid all such people; turn away from them" (2 Tim. 3:1-5, Amp).

It is undeniable that these are the last days. However, many of us in the church do not believe that Jesus will soon come. The signs are clear; we must take heed and not be as the foolish virgins who fell asleep as they were waiting for the bridegroom to return. They did not prepare themselves before the call was made. We must be alert, giving strict attention and caution, being active while expecting his return.

How is it, as people of God, that we could discern many things, whether we will get a house, car or financial blessing, but we cannot discern what's about to happen in the Kingdom of God? Here is a caveat: one day soon there will be a shout, and we must be sure we have oil in our vessels and that our lamps are burning brightly. There will be no time to adorn ourselves with the proper attire for the wedding ceremony. There will be no time to remove our masks.

Chapter 1
Learned Behavior

All my life I've been in church. I have childhood memories of waking up early on Sunday morning to my mother dressing all five of her children, along with specific instructions to sit on the couch and not move until she too was dressed. I remember my sister's and my hair being pressed hard the night before then adorned with ribbons that matched our dresses. Our Charlie Brown black patent leather shoes sparkled in the sun, with matching pocketbooks and gloves. My brother's suit was pressed and creased well, with his tie matching the hardly-noticeable pinstripe. His shoes were buffed until he could see himself and us, too. Everything had to be perfect, for we were going to the House of the Lord.

When we got to church I saw other well-dressed families. Mothers balanced sculptured works of art on their heads, some with feathers and flowers, others so wide that no one could sit next to them. Those that were not dressed to kill were dressed in crisp, white, starched uniforms, with white polished shoes, gloves in hand and sashes draped around one shoulder and pinned at the hip, proudly signifying which usher board they represented. Then, there were the choir robes—long and two-toned with extra fabric for swaying to the music.

I have many fond memories of growing up in church. But one of the things I remember vividly is how the sun would shine gloriously on Sunday morning, melting away any imperfection. I was not like other children who grumbled about Sundays. I looked forward to those perfect days mainly because things weren't so perfect the rest of the week. Sometimes there would be a lot of yelling at my house on Saturday nights after my Dad drank too much. My mother would cry, and we would too. But on Sunday morning as we piled inside the station wagon, we were all perfectly aglow.

This taught me early that going to church required a certain image. Even though we were going to church to "lay our burdens down," no one was to see what kind of burdens they were, and we were supposed to look fine in the process. My mother would remind us that anything coming out of her house had to look good. After all, we were representing her. I wondered if the other mothers had this same rule, because all of the children in the Cherub Choir standing alongside me were also "representing."

From a very early age we all have learned in some way to hide our imperfections. We are told not to cry, not to show our true feelings, and never to tell *all* our business. We were all taught shame. This is not something we are born with; this is a learned behavior. And because of it, we are careful never to release our failures. We cover up any indiscretion, and we disguise our truths.

Chapter 2

The Cost of Being Uncovered

I wrote this book over the course of two years while my family and I were experiencing the worst winter season we could have ever imagined. In the year 2000, while most people were celebrating the new millennium, I was fighting for my survival. My husband and I, after 10 years of marriage, lost everything. We were laid off our jobs and very quickly used what little savings we had. We had been operating a small retail business and because of some bad decisions, went bankrupt. As a result, we were evicted from our home, our car was repossessed, and we had no money. We were homeless, had nowhere to go, and no money to get there. Even though I was in such a state I was too ashamed to let anybody know. I hid behind this shame for over a year. I knew that God was with me no matter what. I knew that whatever I would go through was not just for me alone but so that God could get glory out of my life. Between the tears and constant moves from place to place, I kept hearing the Lord say, "write, write down your experience; write about your process." So I cried, I moved, and I wrote. I did not understand it at the time, but writing down what I went through was therapeutic for me.

During this time, I cried out to God for direction and clarity, but there were no answers. In those two years, we bounced between family, friends and hotels. Everything we owned was in garbage bags and suitcases. We were forced to put our furniture in storage but because we couldn't keep up with the storage fees, all of our possessions were auctioned off to the highest bidder. I still wear the scars on my heart when I think of all the photographs that can never be replaced. Whatever we did not lose in storage we had already sold to the pawn dealer so that we could have enough money for one more night at whatever hotel we managed to find. TVs, VCRs, and cameras were sold so we could have shelter. One day we pawned my wedding rings so we could feed our children. My mink coat was sold in a feeble attempt to put a deposit on an apartment. However, it didn't work out because our credit was so horrible nobody wanted to take a chance. Every time we had to move we would load up the car with our garbage bags and suitcases and ask God to tell us where to go. I was so tired of moving, living out of bags, and sleeping on the floor that I almost lost my mind.

My husband and I performed our daily routine that included filling out applications, going on interviews, going to social services to apply for food stamps and housing, finding our next meal, and securing a place to sleep at night. All of this had to be done before the children were dismissed from school. We never wanted them to worry, so we hid as much from them as we could. I would never go into the social service office; I was too proud. I was still the diva…a homeless diva but a diva, nevertheless.

One day while we were driving along the interstate at about 55mph, the devil began to speak to my mind. "Why don't you open the door and jump out while the car is moving?" He probed, "look, make sure another car is coming behind you so that when you jump out the other car will hit you and there would be no chance of your survival." I could not stand it anymore, so I started screaming. I screamed relentlessly and kicked the dashboard and windows. I kicked, screamed, and yelled until I was numb. George pulled the car over and made a feeble attempt to comfort me, but I had no feeling and was exhausted. I became so numb that I didn't talk or eat. I just wanted to die. I was having a nervous breakdown. I could not and would not accept my realities, so soon I plummeted into depression. My mind could not grasp what was happening to me. My mind could not wrap around the fact that I was serving the Lord, preaching the gospel, and was homeless.

All I wanted was to guard my children through this, whatever *this* was. *This* was no way for children to live. *This* happened to other people not to me. Surely, *this* was not God. *This* had to be the devil. I had never experienced any such thing before. I begged God to take us out of it... if not for me for my children. If not for me, then for His name's sake, but things just grew worse. Little did I know that this was the season for my faith to be tried and proven by fire.

I realized that I had prayed for God to guard my children. I had prayed for the strength of my husband, but I had not prayed for myself. My focus was on staying covered; it was more important for me to mask myself. I had entered into a place of unrest, and the Word of God didn't make sense to me anymore. I could not hear God. I knew His voice, but He was not speaking. I was confused, hurt, heartbroken, and forsaken. Why was this happening to me? What did I do or didn't do to warrant this? What kind of God would let the wicked prosper and the righteous go forsaken? I knew others who had lost their jobs but didn't lose everything. I knew those who squandered and cheated but never received *this* punishment. I began to tell God how good I was—how this shouldn't be my portion. I told Him that He had made a mistake. Maybe He had gotten me confused with somebody else. I'm the one that was always the good girl, the one who never gave my mother trouble. The one who served Him since the age of 13 and prayed until everybody in my whole house knew Him. I am the one that witnessed on the street corners, passed out tracts, and won souls to His kingdom. I'm the one who always went out of my way to help, always wanting to do the right thing and was too scared to do wrong. I am the one who believed that if you were faithful, God would not forget your labor of love.

I believed—and still do—that God will reward faithfulness. Hence, I attended church faithfully, worked in ministry faithfully, and gave my all faithfully. My relationship with God had been of such: I work for You, and You work for me. I declare it, stand back, and watch Him perform it. I named it, claimed it, and had it. I walked with no fear. The agreement had been that I serve God, He blesses me, and we are cool.

A Deeper Relationship

But God was silent. He was changing the script on me. There were no answers and because I was not used to the silence, I slipped into a state of depression. I did not know that even in the silence He speaks. I did not know that if I allowed myself to be still I would hear Him, and that even when He was not saying anything He was speaking volumes. I was not aware that there are times God creates seasons of shortage…times when He will close doors of opportunity and remove all those who represent "help." This is so He can do something awesome and get the credit. I also did not know that He removes all options from your life so that you cannot go backward; you are forced to go forward.

I was dangerously depressed but so bound by pretense that I did not let anyone know. Help was available to me but I would have had to unmask myself to get it. I would go to church and make sure that no one knew we were destitute. I put on my best garments and ensured that nothing would reveal my secret. I smiled and greeted the saints as usual. I said "amen" to the preacher and shouted and danced when the time came. I tried to forget, if not for just a little while. But all the while the devil was tormenting my mind. After service was over, I would go back to my hotel room and crawl into bed, barely moving until the next performance. Every week I would come to the pool and because I was afraid of what people would think of me, I never jumped in. Hence, I was not made whole.

Enough is Enough

In the course of one year my children were registered in three different schools. One morning my son woke up and asked, "Mommy, where are we?" He had forgotten that we had moved during the night, and he had awoken afraid and shaken, not familiar with his surroundings. It was then that my husband and I said "enough." We decided that we were not moving anymore. We picked a town that was known for its excellent school system and checked into one of those hotels that had kitchenettes so that we would be able to cook. For the next year, we called this place home. At least this would help us provide stability for the children. There were other families staying at this hotel temporarily while their homes were being built from the ground. This move allowed me to hide further because people assumed the same about us. I never said we were having a house built from the ground, but I never said we weren't either. I just let people think whatever they wanted to think. I don't even know why I cared what these strangers thought. They didn't know me, yet I cared. I cared about what everyone thought.

The school bus picked the kids up from the hotel every day. They enjoyed the consistency and soon had new friends. But eventually, my children were laughed at and teased by the other kids on the school buses. "Is this where you live?" they were often asked. I remember my children coming home in tears after such episodes. We even had bus drivers who told them that picking them up was an inconvenience that caused everyone to be late. I began to pray, "God, guard my children from bitterness and hardness of heart." I'd taught them from the womb that God was and is everything we needed. I'd taught them that with God nothing is impossible. Even in this struggle, I reaffirmed their faith and wiped every tear away. I reminded God of His promises and told Him He had to keep His word because my children were expecting Him to. Yet I was not so sure.

After September 11, 2001, the economy and the nation suffered great devastation. I continued to look for work and could find nothing. If you didn't already have a job, it was very difficult to get one. Every door that I knew to be opened was closed. I was blinded by what I was experiencing. I was so busy looking at the fact that I was laid off that I didn't realize God had been divinely orchestrating my path. Later, I considered that I probably would have been at the World Trade Center on that dreadful day had I not been laid off. For over seven years, I had worked at the World Financial Center that was connected to the WTC. Every day I commuted on the trains underneath the WTC buildings. On that dreadful day, I would have been getting off the trains approximately the same time that the planes hit the towers. Today, there are no trains and buildings, only a site that reminds me of the goodness of the Lord.

Remember Job's Wife

My husband George managed to find odd jobs to sustain us. He worked day and night to pay the hotel bill and buy food. In order to survive, we lived off the graces of family, friends, and food pantries. George kept reminding the children and me that this was only a season and that soon it would be over. "What's important," he would say, "is that we have each other." *What?* I would get so angry with him for saying that. "It's all going to work out Teri; you'll see." I would watch him work two—sometimes—three jobs day and night, every day of the week. He had no days off. Sometimes he had to walk to work because we didn't have a vehicle. It would seem like every time he had to walk, it would rain. Many nights I sat up worrying that he would be killed and left for dead on the side of the road. I watched the news and waited for the phone to ring, looking for a broadcast that he was dead and I was left alone with the children. I thought this could not be happening to me. This is a dream or, the very least, a movie on Lifetime. He would come home fatigued. Signs of stress had become evident: his skin was darker, and his hair was thinning. Yet he would say each day, "Teri, *this* is only a season; it's all going to work out. God blessed us before and He will bless us again. It's just a season; it will not last always." I hated him. I hated his faith. I hate his hope. I hated his strength. I wanted to scratch his eyes out. We were homeless! Didn't he know that we were homeless? Yet he had the nerve to tell me about seasons? I felt the spirit of Job's wife welling up in me. How can he say everything is going to work out? Doesn't he see where we are? I'm living in a hotel room with my son and daughter sleeping together, and my clothes are in garbage bags. This is not how he met me. I was fine before he came along. I was wonderful all by myself. It's his fault; yeah, that's why he's so jubilant because he knows he's the reason we are in this mess in the first place. Look at him praying…he better pray. He knew he couldn't take care of me. He should have left me where I was. I was doing fine without him. Shoot! He must be crazy if he thinks I'm going to stay here until my hair falls out! I hated that George trusted God and I did not. One day I said to him, "Why are you working so hard? It's been two years and nothing has changed. Let's stop fooling ourselves. If anything were going to happen, it would have happened by now. Nothing is working out because God has forgotten about us. We did something to make Him mad. I don't know what we did. But if He's mad at me, I'm going to be mad at Him too." George said, "Girl stop talking crazy. What are you saying? We can't give up now. Watch and see; God will work it out. He promised He would and He can't lie. We haven't lost everything; we still have each other. The kids are healthy, we are not on the street, and we have food to eat. Teri, we already have everything we need."

Chapter 3
The Mask of Depression

I was reading the newspaper one morning and the headlines read, "Woman throws girls from roof then Jumps." The story said that she was at family court because she had fallen on hard times and was unable to take care of her children sufficiently. The courts had stepped in and were contemplating putting the children in foster care. While the woman waited for her fate, she decided death was the only way out. She went up to the roof of the court building, dropped each of her children, and then jumped.

As I read the article, my eyes welled up with tears. I wondered what lie had this woman assumed. What burden of pretense had she been carrying that finally rendered her unable to cope with life's realities? Was it one that described a perfect family…one with a house and white picket fence? Did she imagine greeting her husband at the door after a hard day's work, with dinner and a freshly baked apple pie?

I wept for this woman and for myself. Not many days before I, too, had contemplated suicide. This time I had thoughts not just of killing myself but also of taking my husband and children with me. But these thoughts were masked from everyone. No one knew that I had slipped so far away. No one knew that I was suffocating behind my mask.

Depression, Numbness, Suicide

Depression is a demonic spirit that renders a person mentally and emotionally helpless. Have you ever read the paper or watched the news and heard of someone taking his/her life in a dreadful way? You think, "My God, how could they have done such a dreadful thing?" I used to say the same thing until I too experienced the numbness of depression.

Numbness is defined as lack of feeling, lack of sensation, deadness. I remember the numbness I felt day in and day out in my hotel room as I waited for change to come. That's why I could identify with the woman who killed herself and her children. Once you become numb it is a stronghold that is not easily broken. This is what the enemy is counting on; he wants you to stay in the state of depression long enough to become numb. When you do, you become capable of doing anything because you no longer *feel* anything. It is this numbness that is perilous. Your mind and body become numb. You feel as if you are dead already. So what if you jump off the roof? You won't feel it. So what if you blow your head off? You won't feel it!

Don't Just Kill Yourself

As the weeks turned into months and years without any change to my situation, I thought God was playing a trick on me. It all seemed like a game, and I was in no mood to play. The enemy wreaked havoc in my mind. I woke every day with headaches, and instead of saying, "thank you Jesus for another day," I was angry that I did not die in my sleep. Another day to me meant struggle and pain. Suicidal thoughts constantly plagued my mind. I had trouble sleeping, for unrest tormented me. Death seemed like the only relief.

I remember lying in my bed one morning while my family slept. I heard a voice say, "turn on the gas and it will all be over." I thought, "Don't just kill yourself; kill everybody, and no one will be left to grieve." I began to reason. If I killed myself, my husband and children would be left with years of dealing with the trauma. If I killed the children and myself, my husband will never understand and would probably blame himself. The only answer was to kill everybody. Then when our bodies would have been found, they'd think it was an accident. This made perfect sense to me. Or so I thought. But these were not my thoughts; the devil was speaking, and I was listening. That is how the devil operates. If you give him room, he will not only speak to your mind, but he will make sense.

Graciously, God kept my mind and came to my rescue. God told my Spiritual Mother, Pastor Mary what the enemy was trying to do to me. She summoned me to her office. I will never forget that Wednesday night because it was the moment of my deliverance. I especially remember that night because there was no reason for me to be at church, so I had to make a sacrifice to get there. This is the way God operates. In order for deliverance to take place, a sacrifice will have to be made. In order for man to be delivered from the sentence of death,

Jesus had to make a sacrifice. So I had to press my way. I had made up my mind that whatever she wanted I was going to say "yes" and "no" and be out of there in a few minutes.

No sooner had I walked into Pastor's office than she said, "Teri, I'm not going to let you die." *What?* "If I have to lay you down, get on top of you, and breathe life back into your body, I will." *What?* Her words took me by surprise. She spoke with authority and arrested the spirit that had become a stronghold in my mind. I began to cry. She interceded and rebuked the enemy that had come to wipe me out. Pastor prayed, "I come against the enemy that has come to destroy you. I take authority over suicidal thoughts and depression. Devil, this is God's child and she has purpose. She will not die but will live and declare the Word of the Lord. What you have brought to destroy her will work together for her good." She continued to speak words of destiny and purpose and told the enemy to back off from me. She began to prophesy to my dry bones and command them to live again. Immediately my spirit was quickened in me, and I was delivered. No more chains holding me! Hallelujah, I'm free!

Chapter 4
The Mask Revealed

After coming out of deep depression, I wondered what I did wrong to fall into such a terrible state. I had moved from being a tongue-talking-Bible-toting-preacher to a confused, suicidal basket case. How did I get this way? I walked with this question in my spirit. I felt such freedom from the heaviness of the mask that I was carrying around. I did not understand why I suffered in silence for so long. Maybe if I had someone I could talk to about what I was going through, this probably would have never happened. I had thought about going to several people but was discouraged by the images portrayed by them and me. Whom could I talk to that was safe? Who would not judge me, talk about me, and make me feel worse than I did? I didn't trust anyone enough. Everyone knew me to be the one that always had it together, and I did not want to be perceived otherwise. It was then that God spoke to me.

Hear the Word of the Lord:

> *Because you are wearing a mask, I cannot deliver you. It is more important to you what people think of you than to be set free from the spirits that are tormenting you. To be set free means to be truthful with yourself and others. You are even willing to die than be exposed. My people are all in need. It is not you only. They all cry out to Me, yet all pretend as if they need nothing. Who I am and what I have done for you is a secret. If My people would dare to reveal their true selves, with all of their shortcomings and failures, I am faithful and able to deliver. When you choose to stay behind your masks, you take on the spirit and the identity of the devil, your forefather, and you can no longer be identified*

as My sons…sons of truth, if you take on the posture of the deceiver. Whom are you fooling? You fool yourselves only. Then are you children of the devil, and you bring life to the plan that the enemy has set up for your lives. In so doing, you fail to let My blood cover you. I cannot protect you if you do not stay under My blood. It is under My blood that you are protected, sheltered, and safe. If you wear the face of the deceiver, you are not under My blood. Take off the masks of bondage. Do not continue to wear a disguise and then cry out to Me to help you. Take off the mask and be set free.

After God spoke this word to me, He began to reveal why I had to continue writing through my experience and process. He told me that I was to write a book and declare this word to the world.

I share this testimony so that you who may be struggling in the area of depression and suicide would be set free. I was delivered so that you would be set free. I know what it is like to continue in the routine just so that you will not bring attention to yourself. I know what it is like to secretly want to die while everyone thinks your life is perfect. I know what it is like to come to church and even function in ministry while your whole life is falling apart. But you must be bold enough to come from behind your mask and pretense. You cannot continue to fake it. When you do this, you are on the devil's territory. He is the master of disguise, and he does not play fair. He is the thief who comes to steal, kill, and destroy.

> Let's pray:
> *I come against the enemy now in the name of Jesus. I curse the devil that has spoken to your mind and has told you that your situation is not going to change. I speak to that devil that has said there is no way out, other than death. Devil, you are a liar and a deceiver. I curse your plan. I curse your works. You are already defeated. I speak God's Word over you now, my sister, that the joy of the Lord shall be your strength. I speak the Word over you today, my brother. You shall not die but live and declare the works of the Lord. I declare that purpose and destiny shall be fulfilled.*

Now rise, pick up your bed, and walk!

Chapter 5
The Masquerade

What is the proper attire for church? Most religious sectors have customs to which they adhere before entering their place of worship. The belief is that one should be adorned properly before one can come to God. For instance, Muslims and Jews are very specific in their dress. At the mosque, the women are covered from head to toe as a sign of submission. The covering of the head symbolizes humility, acknowledging someone greater. Then, there is the practice of the Catholics to sprinkle themselves with holy water in the sign of the cross before they enter their sanctuaries.

For years we have argued who is right. Several of us are still debating whether women should wear earrings, makeup, and pants. In our debate, we have lost sight of the vocation to which we are called. We have turned our focus towards the adorning of our flesh rather than the adorning of our spirits.

We come to our places of worship fully dressed and unwilling to be disclosed, as if it were a masquerade. We attend in well-thought-out costumes that are deliberately designed to distract attention from the bruises and scars that life has left behind. We have masked our realities by adorning ourselves. The more expensive our clothes, the less attention we bring to our true selves. We give others the perception that everything is "blessed" because we *appear* to be blessed. Just as a woman who wouldn't go out of the house without her face (makeup) on, we church folk would not dare leave home without our masks. We reach for our masks just as we reach for our Bibles as we walk out the door. Our behaviors teach that you can only approach God when you have it all together. We communicate that you cannot come to church with needs, imperfections, or insecurities. As long as we continue to perpetuate this lie, true redemption cannot take place. Our intent is not to fool God. We are clear that we cannot do that, for He is omniscient. However, it is more important for us to fool one another.

Our churches have become places where hypocrites, not worshippers, gather. We pretend like we have it together and have always had it together, but if the truth were told we would have to admit we've gotten into some real messes since we've been saved. We are faithful hypocrites who attend church week after week, never removing the masks. We never let anyone know that we weren't born holy. We never leak out that the same struggles they are facing we too have been through or are going through. We never let anyone in, never let anyone know who we really are or what Jesus has saved us from.

Unwed mothers, battered wives, AIDS victims, and the homeless stumble into our churches not knowing the learned etiquette of the day. They come in without their masks, revealing bruises, nakedness, and scars. Sometimes they smell and are not properly dressed. This has become offensive to us. We do not sit next to them, and we dare not sit them in the front of the church because they may cause distraction. Instead, they are thrust to the back of the church where they can be watched by security. What is their crime? Only that they are without masks! They did not know that they had entered a masquerade; they did not know they should have come in costume.

In the name of tradition, I have seen young women with swollen bellies placed on the front row and/or put in front of the congregation…the products of promiscuity. Tradition demands that we take the young woman and make an example of her so that other girls will not make the same mistake. Instead of tradition's speaking words of experience, lessons in how not to fall into the snares of the enemy, the young girl is made to swim in a pool of shame, paddled by guilt. No lifeline is thrown to her because our belief is that she deserves punishment for her sin. Nobody bothers to consider that she has made a decision not to abort her baby while others—even among the team of accusers—are equally or more guilty.

In the fullness of time, after her sin has matured and can no longer be contained, it is born in the pool in which it was developed—shame. Now begins another generation of low self-esteem and low self-worth. No wonder those girls that have watched this "example" *still* choose to abort so that they will not endure the same disdain.

We have become as the Pharisees who knew the law and were quick to point fingers and pass judgment, but their hearts were far from God.

Jesus rebuked them. *"You set yourselves up to judge according to the flesh by what you see. You condemn by external, human standards. I do not set myself up to judge or condemn or sentence anyone" (John 8:15, Amp).*

Elsewhere Jesus advised,

> *"Do not judge and criticize and condemn others, so that you may not be judged and criticized and condemned yourselves...For just as you judge and criticize and condemn others, you will be judged and criticized and condemned, and in accordance with the measure you use to deal out to others, it will be dealt out again to you...Why do you stare from without at the very small particle that is in your brother's eye but do not become aware of and consider the beam of timber that is in your own eye?" (Matt. 7:1-3)*

Maybe I was not promiscuous and you did not have a problem with fornication, but for us to sit piously and behave as if we have never done anything is pretentious and the truth of God is not in us. It was to the accusing men who dragged the adulterous woman that Jesus said,

"...He that is without sin among you, let him first cast a stone..." (John 8:7).

If we don't take off the masks, the cycle will continue. We do our children an injustice by wearing masks. Then, we come to church and declare "amen" to the truth. But what is the truth? Our children know that the mirror has two faces. They know that home is not as sweet as the plaque hanging on the kitchen wall says it is.

We confuse our children as we teach them by example to fake it, to put on a front. Then when our teenagers become of age and begin to kick against the pretenses, we throw our hands up and say that we can't do anything with them. It is not because they don't want to obey. It is not because they don't want to listen. It's because the mask doesn't fit!

Chapter 6
Master of Disguise

When I was growing up as a young girl in church, the mothers would look at us with piercing eyes as if to see if we were still living holy. They thought that we would backslide and sin during the week, so they wanted to know if we were still holding on. They would also look at how we dressed. If they thought our skirts were too short or too tight, they might say we looked like the devil. These women of God put a lot of weight on holiness, holy living, and holy appearances. I concur that holiness is and always will be critical, for God is holy and we who are called by His name must be holy. But some of us have misconstrued holiness by inferring that it is only a look. The notion is that if I look holy, then I am holy.

In one of Jesus' many conversations with the Jews, they claimed that they were descendants of Abraham. Jesus replied,

> *"if you were truly Abraham's children you would do the works of Abraham, follow his example, do as Abraham did. But now instead you are seeking to kill me, a man who has told you the truth, which I have heard from God. This is not the way Abraham acted. You are doing the works of your own father" (John 8:39-41, Amp.).*

Relentlessly, they sought to justify their legitimacy to Abraham's lineage, but to no avail. Jesus continued,

> *"...if God were your Father, you would love me and respect me and welcome me gladly, for I proceeded (came forth) from God out of his very presence. I did not even come on my own authority or of My own accord as self-appointed; but He*

> *sent me. Why do you misunderstand what I say? It is because you are unable to hear what I am saying. You cannot bear to listen to my message; your ears are shut to my teaching. You are of your father, the devil, and it is your will to practice the lusts and gratify the desires, which are characteristic of your father" (vs. 42-44, Amp).*

When I was growing up, my sisters and I would play outside with a bunch of the neighborhood kids. It did not matter how many other kids were there, for occasionally somebody would come over and pick us out of the crowd because we looked like our father. Even when we tried to be slick and get away with something, we would hear, "I know you know better, because I know your father." Hence, whoever and whatever your father is that will you emulate. There's no need in trying to pretend. The character of your father will soon show through.

Likewise, you will not be able to hear and understand the things of God if you are not of God. You may even find yourself saying things like, "It doesn't take all of that." "Why does she have to praise God all the time?" "Why do we have to do it that way?" Sisters and brothers, when you hear your conversation changing in this manner and you begin to question the things of God, you are no longer hearing clearly.

Do not think that you can be deceitful in one area and not in another. If you lie about one thing, you will soon find yourself lying about something else. If you lie on your application, you will have to lie on your interview to cover the lie you told on your application. Then you will have to call up references and ask them to lie as well. If you are a liar in one thing, *"...you are of all that is false" (John 8:44).*

There are several instances in scripture that prove God despises deception. Here are three such examples. Firstly, Genesis 27 tells the story of Jacob and Esau:

Are you really my son Esau? He answered, I am.

Then Isaac proceeds to bless Jacob who deceived him into thinking that he was Esau,

> *Isaac said, your brother came with crafty cunning and treacherous deceit and has taken your blessing. Because of this Esau hated his*

brother Jacob and sought to kill him.

Secondly, Genesis 12 presents Abram's deception that brought about a curse on Pharaoh's house,

> ***"But the Lord scourged Pharaoh and his household with serious plagues because of Sarai, Abram's wife. And Pharaoh called Abram and said, What is this that you have done to me? Why did you not tell me that she was your wife?....Now then, here is your wife; take her and get away (from here)! (vs 17, Amp)***

Thirdly, Proverbs 6:16 declares that there are seven things God hates:

1. a proud look (the spirit that makes one overestimate himself and underestimate others)
2. a lying tongue
3. hands that shed innocent blood
4. a heart that manufactures wicked thoughts and plans
5. feet that are swift in running to evil

6. a false witness who breathes out lies (even under oath)
7. and he who sows discord among his brethren.

Examine the text carefully. Out of the seven things that God hates, two of them are liars.

Chapter 7

Masked in the Pulpit

When I first heard the call to the Ministry, one of the scriptures God spoke to my heart was,

Isaiah 58:1:
"Cry aloud, spare not, lift up thy voice like a trumpet, and shew my people their transgression, and the house of Jacob their sins."

I used this text at my introductory sermon. My subject was "Sound the alarm: It's an emergency!" That was over 18 years ago and throughout the years, whenever I would try to stray away from this message and preach a more popular message—one that would bring me a lot of "amen," one that would make the people dance and shout—I would get into deep trouble with God. So I have learned that I would rather lose friends and give up being popular than fall into the hands of an angry God. I knew that I would make a lot of people mad if I wrote about the mask of ministry. But I told you this message did not come without great cost.

Ministry is one of the greatest areas of deception for the devil. It is one of his biggest hiding places, for homosexuals hide in ministry; whoremongers hide in ministry; pimps hide in ministry; con artists hide in ministry, looking for their next victims; wife beaters and child molesters hide in ministry. They do so very easily because of the mask that says, "because I am in ministry, because I carry a Bible and sit in the pulpit, I am holy.

Apostle Paul writes in Romans 7:

> ***"We know that the Law is spiritual; but I am a creature of the flesh, carnal, unspiritual, having been sold into slavery under the control of sin. For I do not understand my own actions. I am baffled,***

bewildered. I do not practice or accomplish what I wish, but I do the very thing that I loathe, which my moral instinct condemns. Now if I do habitually what is contrary to my desire, that means that I acknowledge and agree that the Law is good, morally excellent and that I take sides with it. However, it is no longer I who do the deed, but the sin, which is at home in me, and has possession of me. For I know that nothing good dwells within me, that is in my flesh. I can will what is right, but I cannot perform it. I have the intention and urge to do what is right, but no power to carry it out. For I fail to practice the good deeds I desire to do but the evil deeds that I do not desire are what I am ever doing. Now if I do what I do not desire to do, it is no longer I doing it, it is not myself that acts, but the sin which dwells within me, fixed and operating in my soul. So I find it to be a law, rule of action, of my being, that when I want to do what is right and good, evil is ever

> *present with me and I am subject to its insistent demands. (14-21, Amp)*

Paul explains that he has no control over his flesh. Even though he desires to do what is right, he has no power of himself to carry it out. He says even if he practiced and rehearsed doing good deeds, that which he hates is what he would do. Hence, we must never trust our flesh. We must crucify our members; we must die to this flesh daily.

I can attest to the lawlessness of the flesh. In my youth I did not know how to control my sexuality. I did not stay focused and was blinded by the need to appease my flesh. The devil tricked me and showed me those who were sexually active, unmarried, and still singing in the choir and in leadership positions. I reasoned with myself that if they could do it so could I.

So when I became pregnant, I hid because I didn't want anyone to know. There was so much shame and disappointment. I finally told George. He was ecstatic and wanted to announce the news. I told him he must not—could not—tell anyone. We would go through with the wedding plans as usual and no one would know I was with child. Though my pretense made George uncomfortable, he conceded...because he loved me.

For six months I hid myself. I am naturally thin, so this was no easy task. I could not wear big shirts because this would have given me away. I wore girdles, and as I got bigger, I wore two girdles. Every day I stuffed my shame. At my wedding, I wore two girdles. Though my wedding pictures showed me with perfect posture, dress and smile, I couldn't breathe. All I cared about was not letting anyone find out until after the wedding. I was bound by what would people say and think.

However, when I returned from the honeymoon, I had a big belly and a smile. No one was fooled! Everybody had known that I was pregnant and wondered what was under my clothes. I felt like a fool.

Throughout the rest of my pregnancy, I wore the weight of guilt, shame, and defeat. Two months later, I was hospitalized and put on bed rest for thirty days. I had fluid in both lungs, and was severely anemic, dehydrated, and underweight. Further testing revealed antibodies for lupus and an enlarged heart that was struggling to keep me alive. It was then I knew that God was trying to get my attention.

Room at the Altar

When I first started in ministry I was told to never let the people see my nakedness. This actually meant to never let people see my need and shortcomings. Ministers were told not to go to the altar at the same time with the congregation. We should seek God privately and separately from the people.

Lies are perpetuated by the notion that ministers are called to give counsel, pray for the sick, feed and shelter the poor, hear confessions, and bid pardon, but *they* themselves should not be in need. If they are, they are not supposed to show it.

Today, ministers are still required to uphold a certain standard of professionalism; therefore, no one should see them out of character. But while this is true, our calling does not exempt us from being human beings. I cannot count how many times a minister confessed to me that he/she wanted so desperately to respond to the altar call but did not because of the image that was required. Because of these images and rules, our clergy are going to hell.

Who ministers to the minister? Where does the minister go for comfort? I believe the congregation needs to see leadership in prayer. As people of influence, we have a great responsibility. We have to show people who look to us the way to God. We must take them to the altar, always showing the Cross of Calvary and, thereby, keeping ourselves grounded. If not, we put ourselves in the position of God, with the people becoming dependent upon us.

This reminds me of a telephone conversation I had with a Christian friend. We will call her Jane. Jane is very glamorous and always put together. She is the type of person that would never be seen without her hairpiece, nails, makeup, and jewelry in place. One day Jane told me that she was embarrassed at the behavior of another Christian sister, Jill. "What behavior?" I asked. Knowing Jill, I became concerned. I hadn't noticed anything wrong or out of the ordinary. Jane said earnestly, "it is disgraceful that Jill runs to the altar every time the altar call is made. She acts so needy, and I don't want to be associated with anyone who is always crying and can't get it together." I wanted to scream in Jane's ear. Instead, my soul has screamed out to God many days since. I told Jane, as calmly as I could, that we couldn't ever forget there is redemption at the altar. I reminded her that we don't have a right to say who goes to the altar and who doesn't. It is a misconception to think that the altar is only for sinners, and that those who have it together don't need to come. Oh, I pray for the day that every altar would be filled with those of us who believe we have it together, because it is at the altar that we will find we do not.

Paul wrote to the saints at Philippi:

> *"Let this mind be in you, which was also in Christ Jesus. Who although being essentially one with God and in the form of God (possessing the fullness of the attributes which make God) did not think this equality with God was to be eagerly grasped. But stripped Himself of all privileges and rightful dignity. So as to assume the guise of a servant (slave) in that He became like men and was born a human being. And after He had appeared in human form, He abased and humbled Himself (still further) and carried his obedience to the extreme of death, even the death of the cross: Therefore, because He stooped so low God has highly exalted him and has freely bestowed to Him the name that is above every name. That at the name of Jesus every*

> ***knee should bow, in heaven and on earth and under the earth. (2:5-10, Amp)***

We have been misinformed if we think the position or the high seat of ministry is the blessing. Crowned heads cannot bow low before God, who is the King of kings. We must remove our titles in His presence so that we can see His face. It is in His presence—not in seminary—that we find promotion. As ministers, we should be the first ones in prayer. We should be the first ones at the altar, the first ones to seek the face of God. Sisters and brothers, He bids us come. Come often and stay longer. Come. Leaders, we have to remain in the posture of prayer. We can do nothing without it. Before we pray for others, let us be found at the altar seeking the face of God. He bids us come.

Snare of False Humility

The Catholic priests who were discovered in sin brought devastation and shock to this great nation. Their vestments were not long enough to cover their deceit. I believe that it was God who pulled the cover and exposed the sin. There is a shaking going on, and we must be aware of the times. Reluctance to repent of sin must be judged, and this ***"judgment must start at the house of God (1 Pet. 4:17).***

When one has been given the awesome charge to speak as an oracle of God, offer the Holy Sacraments, and hear confessions as these priests were, one must be careful not to operate in false humility. The priest must not forget that he/she is mortal and nothing but dust in the sight of God. I speak prophetically to the Christian church also. We must not point fingers, judge, and celebrate the demise of the Catholics. Each of us is guilty, and there is nothing hidden that shall not be revealed (Luke 12:2). We have separated the church into doctrines and legalism, but God is coming back for one church, a prepared people for a prepared place. It is not because these were Catholic priests that they were exposed. It is because they tried to cover sin and deceive the sacred oath of the church. It is because they hid behind the name of God who is holy, continued in their sin, and never repented.

Clearly, the devil is after our leaders. He wants us to lead in false humility. He wants us to teach in falsehood. He wants us to preach one thing and live another. But I declare to you today, that it is the devil who tells you there is no one that will understand what you are going through. Pastor, I don't care how many members you have. It is the devil that is saying you are in too deep to come out. The devil is a liar. The altar is open for you too, preacher, prophet, ministry leader. Restoration is available for you too. True deliverance cannot come to the body unless our pulpits are unmasked. We dare not preach this gospel and we ourselves become cast away (1 Cor. 9:27).

Chapter 8

The Mask of Sickness

I have been in church for a long time and have seen many things. I've seen people die in the church from various sicknesses and diseases because they did not want anyone to know what they were suffering with. While they believe Jesus is the healer, they have allowed the enemy to keep them bound to a mask.

In the 80's, Acquired Immune Deficiency Syndrome (AIDS) became prevalent in our churches. During that time I went to many funerals and heard of many more. People debated whether this was God's wrath upon the homosexual. I saw saints of God actually afraid to touch one another. For a minute, there was no "hug of love" or "holy kissing" in the church. All physical contact ceased. People were genuinely afraid because, at the time, no one knew how AIDS was contracted. I saw it as a cancer like any other parasite that invaded the body. To me, how it got there was not important. Whatever it was, I knew the blood of Jesus could heal it.

Healing Behind the Mask

I remember one brother; we'll call him John. John had AIDS. But John did not care what people thought of him. He did not care about the debate. He did not care if people thought he was homosexual. He knew that he was sick, and the prognosis was death. John took off the mask of pretense and sickness, fell at the altar, and cried out to God. He came to the only One that was able to help him. He came to the only One that could set him free, that could wash him and make him whole. He came to Jesus! Had he listened to the people who were talking, he would have stayed behind his mask and died, like so many others.

Taking off the mask was not easy for John, for when he removed his mask, we saw awful lesions on his face and hands. He was not pleasant to look at. People did not want to shake his hand or embrace him, but John kept coming to church. And when he came into the house of God, he came with praise. John would dance before the Lord, lesions and all. And right before my eyes, I watched God heal John, in the praise. Hallelujah!

Still there was another brother, Steve. Steve had AIDS also. Steve never said he had AIDS, but the symptoms were clear, just as they were with John. Steve constantly worried about what people thought rather than making sure he was in right relationship with God. This was a man who was very handsome and well dressed. He was a David in God's house. He sang until it seemed like shackles were being loosed. God had prospered him and he traveled all over the world and sang before great men. He soon took on a pious spirit, began to rely on himself, and did not remain pure before God. Steve wore a mask of pride. He was taken in sin and did not have a repentant heart. He became deathly ill but continued to sing and travel, determined to prove to everyone that he was not sick. When he became too sick to come to church, he concerned himself with what he thought people were saying about him. When I called to see how he was doing, he always wanted to know what this one was saying and what that one was saying. Steve never came to the altar for healing. He was too concerned with what people would think if he went to the altar. I saw the devil strip him down to skin and bones and then cover his eyes to his own nakedness. Only the devil will lead you into sin and then render you helpless, exposing you for all to see. Only the devil will force you out of your father's house, strip you of your position, use you up, then leave you crawling in the mud with pigs (Luke 15:15-16).

Just as the altar was open for John, it was for Steve. However, Steve never removed the mask, and he died. He wore the mask until his death. Though he had access to the Father and the opportunity to be healed, he didn't want to remove his mask. Steve was bound by people.

One of the greatest deliverances you can ever experience is to be delivered from people. If you ever get to the place where you don't care what people think of you and you don't care what people say about you, you have already won half the battle in your Christian journey. Some of us stay in abusive relationships because we would rather stay than have everybody think we are not the perfect couple. Others hold on to images of success, drive cars they can't afford, and live in houses they can't pay for, just so people would say they are blessed.

You must get to the place where all you want is God, where nothing else matters to you. You must get to the place where you are willing to do anything, look funny, be ridiculed, and/or be called a fanatic, as long as you please God. When you get to that place, you will discover that you won't have many friends and you won't be very popular. Pleasing God has to be the only thing that matters to you. I challenge you to obey God rather than man. I challenge you to dare to be talked about just so that God would be glorified. I challenge you to take off the mask and be naked before Him.

Sisters and brothers, if you are sick, do not believe the lie that says you must have sinned and you deserve it. Sickness is of the devil; it is not from God. Remove the mask of sickness. Tell Jesus what you are suffering with and watch Him heal you.

Masked Wombs

It is my belief that fibroid tumors are the result of suppressed pain and suppressed issues. A lot of women walk around with unforgiveness and pent up anger. When these emotions are not dealt with and released, they form tumors. These fibroids are products of things that we have tucked neatly behind our masks, and now they are festering cancers in our bodies. Fibroids cluster in the womb, killing off the ability to produce life. The womb of the woman is an incubator; it is where life is formed and seed is planted. Men are the planters. Man plants the seed into the womb, and the woman nurtures that seed. Then in time she gives birth to that which was planted inside of her.

Men are also visionaries. God gives man the vision, and man gives the vision to woman. She will then carry it and, in the fullness of time, give birth to the vision. This is why the woman must be careful about what she accepts because whatever she gets she will multiply. If the man gives the woman a seed, she will give him a baby. If he gives her a vision, she will manifest the dream. If he gives her a house, she will give him a home. If he gives her some groceries, she will make him a meal.

So then, it is important that wombs be healed. When a woman desires to get pregnant, she usually gets a check up to ensure that she is healthy enough to bring a baby to term. After many test are done, she is given the green light to get pregnant. As it is in the natural, so it is in the spiritual. We cannot give life to visions and dreams if we are not whole, from the inside out. We will miscarry or give birth prematurely because our wombs are not healed.

That's why it is the trick of the enemy for us to continue to hide behind masks and not be fully delivered. He knows that if we are delivered, we will give birth to what the world has been waiting for. If he kills our womb, he kills off the source through which life is formed. If he kills our wombs, he kills visions, dreams, and purpose. The enemy attacks marriages because he does not want seed planting to take place. His plan is to stop our destiny from ever being planted. When he does this, he cuts off our purpose before it gets started. God told Jeremiah that before he was in his mother's womb, God knew him (Jeremiah 1:5). This implies that each of us has purpose that was determined while we were yet seed form.

Chapter 9
Unmask Your Need

My people are all in need. It is not you only.
They all cry out to me.
And yet all pretend as if they need nothing.

It is a form of rejection when we are not willing to admit that we need God. That is what we are saying when we pretend we need nothing. In our closets we cry out to God for help. But when we come out, we behave as if we have it all together. Then, when the requests are met, because we were not willing to tell anyone of the need, glory is not given to God. Don't let the devil trick you into thinking that people just want to know your business. If you would search your Bibles, you would find that every person who was touched by Jesus first identified his/her need before deliverance came. The Bible records that there was a leper, a man possessed by the devil, a blind man, and a woman with an issue of blood. Their needs were identified then Jesus ministered to the need.

Everybody has needs and desires. Everybody has experienced failure. Someone once said that you never really experience success until you have experienced failure. I remember when God was unmasking me. I was sitting in the pulpit, and I knew everybody knew what I was going through. My husband and I were quickly removed from the A list to the Z list. When we used to get invited to parties and fellowships, the phone stopped ringing and no invitations were sent. The word was out that we didn't have anywhere to live and we were the talk of the town. Tears rolled down my face as I complained to God. "Why did everybody have to know what I was going through? Why did I have to be made ashamed? I already told You I would serve You, preach Your Word, and obey. Now, You have me naked before Your people, stripped so that everyone could see my failures, in a high seat where there is no covering. Why did I have to move out of my comfort zone to this desert place where I am all alone?" God's eventual reply was, "I've done this so that all will know it was I who brought you out, and for your shame I will give you double."

Attribution

Sisters and brothers, do not let what God has done for you be a secret. God will allow you to go through openly so that He can openly bless you. God wants us to be witnesses to the world, declaring to everyone all that He is in our lives. Somebody is waiting to hear your testimony. Somebody needs to hear what you have been through. Somebody needs to hear that you survived by the grace of God. Greater glory would be given to God if we would speak of the process that it took us to get to the blessing. We would have people believe that the blessing came easily. But in order to receive anything that is of great value it will have to cost something. Why not give testimony to the cost so that others will know that what they are experiencing is investment towards the greater blessing to come?

The miracle was not that the people of Israel made it to the Promised Land. The miracle was that they did not die in the wilderness. The woman with the issue of blood…her miracle was not that she touched Jesus and was made whole. Her miracle was that she survived twelve years of hemorrhaging. Sisters and brothers, unmask your need today, and let it give glory to God!

Chapter 10
Naked and not Ashamed

Shame and insecurities are reasons that we mask ourselves. The media bombards us with images of big houses, expensive cars, designer clothes, and bling bling. These things are defined as success, and they become the reasons we mask ourselves if we do not have them. However, it was not God's intent for man to live like this.

The Bible says,

> *"Adam and Eve were both naked and were not ashamed or embarrassed in each other's presence" (Gen. 2:25, Amp).*

The word *naked* here can be replaced with *transparent.* Adam and Eve were both transparent and not ashamed. This suggests that God's original intent was for us to be transparent—without inhibitions, insecurities, or shame. We were created with authority, dominion, and power.

In Genesis 3:5, Satan insinuated great improvements Adam and Eve would make by eating the fruit.

1. *Your eyes shall be opened.* This speaks of blindness. God made man in His image and there was nothing lacking or missing.
2. *You shall be as gods.* How absurd! As if it is possible for the creature to be equal to his creator.
3. *You shall know good and evil.* This implies that God is keeping something from them.

What Adam and Eve failed to realize was that they were already like God. They already had everything they needed. There was nothing they could not have. There was nothing they could not do. They had authority over ever living thing in creation, yet they did not know this.

It is not what you are that's holding you back; it is what you think you are not. The weapon of deception is to maintain ignorance in you. If you ever accept the truth about you, you will never accept the lie that the devil tells about you. The truth is that you are more than a conqueror. You can do all things through Christ. Why should you stay behind a mask and perpetuate a lie when you can take off the mask and live the truth?

Deception: Result of Disobedience

> *"And when the woman saw that the tree was good for food and that it was delightful to look at, and a tree to be desired in order to make some wise, she took of its fruit and ate. Then the eyes of them both were opened, and they knew that they were naked: and they sewed fig leaves together and made themselves apronlike girdles. The eyes of them were both opened and they knew that they were naked" (Gen. 3:6-7).*

In this text, the word ***naked*** takes on a different meaning than in Genesis 2:25. Here the word means *unprotected, uncovered,* or *exposed.* This connotation assumes shame.

Here is theologian Matthew Henry's comment on the text.

> *Now Adam and Eve saw the happiness they had fallen from, and the misery they had fallen into. They saw a loving God provoked, His grace and favor forfeited, His likeness and image lost, dominion over the creatures gone. They saw their natures corrupted and depraved, and felt a disorder in their own spirits of which they had never before been conscious. They were forever shamed, before God and the angels. They saw themselves disrobed of all their ornaments, degraded from their dignity and disgraced in the highest degree, laid open to the contempt and reproach of heaven, earth, and their own consciences. They knew that they were stripped, deprived of all the honors and joys of their paradise*

state, and exposed to all the miseries that might justly be expected from an angry God. They were disarmed; their defense had departed from them.

God Called You

"And they heard the sound of the Lord God walking in the garden in the cool of the day, and Adam and his wife hid themselves from the presence of the Lord God among the trees of the garden. But the Lord God called to Adam and said to him where are you?" (Gen. 3:8-9) God was not just asking where Adam was because He knew exactly where he was. Instead, God was asking Adam what condition was he in. Where was he in relationship to God?

Just as my Pastor had called me to her office that day, God is calling you. He is not calling because He does not know where you are but because He wants to know where you are in your relationship with Him. It was God who spoke to my Pastor to call me on that day. God knew that the enemy was about to overtake me. God knew exactly what I needed. I would have rather stayed concealed, dying in deception. If God had not called me, I probably would have been in a padded cell with my arms tied behind my back.

Those of you who have gone astray from God should seriously consider where you are. You are afar from all good. You are in the bondage of Satan and on your way to destruction. But even in your sin, God pursues you. *Where are you Adam?* If God had not called to reclaim Adam, his condition would have been as desperate as that of fallen angels. If the Good Shepherd had not gone after him, Adam would have wandered endlessly. God's call and pursuit reminded Adam of where he ought to have been.

Naked and Hidden

When Adam heard the sound of God in the garden, he was afraid and hid himself. Who would think it possible to hide from God? How could one conceal himself from the Father of light? However, with disobedience comes sin, and that with shame. Then, the immediate response is to cover oneself. The next time you find yourself hiding your insecurities and masking your needs, look in the mirror and ask yourself, "Who told you that you were naked? Who told you that to be naked was to be ashamed? Who told you that when I created you in My likeness and image you were not perfect?" People of God, we were created to be fearless, transparent, and unashamed.

The only reason to be afraid of approaching God is if we are not clothed and fenced with the righteousness of Christ. Nothing but righteousness will be armor of proof to cover the shame of our nakedness.

Chapter 11
Covered by the Blood

When we take off our masks, we allow the redemptive blood of Jesus to cover us. Did you know that without the blood of Jesus covering you, God could not even look at you? Prophet Isaiah declares, *"...your iniquities have separated between you and your God, and your sins have hid his face from you, that he will not hear" (59:2).*

The blood of Jesus allows us access to the Father. Without it we could never be righteous enough to stand in the presence of Almighty God. All of the fixing up and cleaning up we do would never make us clean enough to stand in His presence, without the blood of His Son covering us.

When we come to God, He sees the blood of His Son and is reminded of the promise to redeem man. He is reminded of Jesus' selfless act of obedience to give up His deity and become our Passover lamb. Paul confirms that, *"Christ has redeemed us from the curse of the law, having become a curse for us." (Gal. 3:13, Amp)*

What we are saying when we hide behind masks is that the blood of Jesus is not enough to cover us and that God's redemptive plan is fallible. When we wear masks, we take our lives out of the hands of God and tell Him that we have a better way. This is dangerous! When you take yourself out of the covering of the blood of Jesus, you remove yourself from safety.

Hear what God spoke to me:

"I cannot protect you if you do not stay under My blood. It is under My blood that you are protected, sheltered, and safe. If you wear the face of the deceiver, you are not under My blood."

Benefits of the Blood

Only the blood of Jesus can offer the proper compensation for sin. Lev 17:11 records, *"For the life of the flesh is in the blood: and I have given it to you upon the altar to make an atonement for your souls: for it is the blood that maketh an atonement for the soul."*

The blood covers mistakes. Hebrews 9:7 reads,

"But into...went the high priest alone once every year, not without blood with him, which he offered for himself, and for the errors of the people."

Later in the book of Hebrews, the scribe records,

> *"For when every command of the Law had been read out by Moses to all the people, he took the blood of slain calves and goats, together with water and scarlet wool and with a bunch of hyssop, and sprinkled both the Book and all the people,*
> *Saying these words: This is the blood that seals and ratifies the agreement, the covenant which God commanded me to deliver to you.*

And in the same way he sprinkled with the blood both the tabernacle and all the sacred vessels and appliances used in divine worship. In fact under the Law almost everything is purified by means of blood, and without the shedding of blood there is neither release from sin and its guilt nor the remission of the due and merited punishment for sins." (9:19-22)

Get Covered; Stay Covered

God speaks this same word today. He is coming, and when He does, His righteousness will be so great that it will smite the unjust. Those of us who want to be saved must stay under the blood of Jesus Christ. Some of us may have done terrible things in our lifetime, but as long as we get under the covering of the blood of Jesus, we will be safe. It is when we remove ourselves that we become exposed to the wrath of the soon-coming King. When we remove ourselves, we fail to be prepared for the Bridegroom.

The Bible says that Jesus will come to the earth twice, once as Savior and the other as Judge. Scriptures record the history of the Savior. Now, we await the Judge. When Jesus returns, He will recognize only His blood. He will take with Him only those who are covered with His seal. Woe, then, to those who would have covered themselves with pretenses, fine clothing, and education, instead of with the blood of the Lamb!

Sisters and brothers, I admonish you to get covered and stay covered. It's the devil's job to trick you to step out from under the blood. Some of us play with the devil and stick our toes out every once in a while. But I would not play games with my eternity, for "...***no one knows the day or hour that the Son of man will come" (Matt. 24:36).***

Matthew Henry's comments:

> *The blood and water that flowed out of Jesus' side at the crucifixion was significant in that it distinguished the two great benefits, which all believers can partake, justification and sanctification. The blood of Jesus sanctifies us; it sets us apart for His use. The blood of Jesus justifies us. It says even though we deserve punishment, He will pardon. The blood for remission, and water for regeneration, blood for atonement, and water for purification. The blood covers our sin, and the water washes away all guilt.*

Chapter 12

Trust God

Child of God, you will experience great frustration unless you submit to God's timetable and rip up your own. I am not suggesting that God will not fulfill your dreams and give you your heart's desire. It just may not happen when or how you think it should. Life requires us to be resilient. There are many things that will come your way that will require you to make adjustments. Life itself is full of adjustments. If you are the type of person that has to have everything exactly as planned and are not willing to adapt, you are in for trouble. Just like a tree that bends to the commands of the wind, we must also learn how to bend in the storms of life. If we do not, we will be like the tree that—after the tempest ceased—perished under the pressure because its roots were not secure. Taking off the mask means trusting God with your life. That's easier said than done!

Trust the Plan

I was devastated when I lost my home and possessions because I had been trying to choose my process. While I believed God for the promise, I despised the process. I hated it so much that I masked myself in it and almost forfeited God's promises. What I was trying to hold onto was not my destiny; God had something greater. I was asking God for greatness but was not willing to give up the mediocre. God knows what it's going to take to get you to where He needs you to be. When He takes us through the process, He is grooming, purging, enabling, and equipping us. Could it be that God was setting me up to receive more than I could ever ask or think?

When you mask yourself in the process, you're telling God that you are ashamed of what He is choosing to do and the way He is choosing to do it. You are limiting your prosperity, success, and destiny. In order to receive the blessings of God, you must trust the plan of God.

You don't get to choose your testimony

No matter how much I resisted my process, I have since learned that you don't get to pick your testimony. I don't care how long you've been saved or how close of a relationship you think you have with God. You don't get to choose the process that will allow His promise to be revealed. We don't get to choose our testimony. If we could, I would have chosen the one that would not have required me to lose everything. I would have chosen one that included great miracles and revelation. I would have picked one that did not require suffering and pain. But, alas, we do not get to choose!

Joseph's Process

How can we talk about process and promise and not think of Joseph? In Genesis 37:7, Joseph shares his dream with his brothers. ***"We (I and my brethren) were binding sheaves in the field, and behold, my sheaf arose and stood upright, and behold, your sheaves stood round about my sheaf and bowed down."*** This was Joseph's promise. However, in his zeal, Joseph did not wait for a better revelation of the dream. Instead, he ran to his brothers and told them of the vision. He soon wished that he had kept it to himself because his brothers ventured to kill him. This was the beginning of Joseph's process.

Thirteen years passed between the promise and the process, during which Joseph was thrown into a pit, sold into slavery, jailed, then placed in the King's palace. This was all the plan of God. How could that be the plan of God? Many of us don't believe that some things are not the plan of the devil but, instead, are divinely orchestrated by God. Some things that you are experiencing…yes, that thing that is pushing you into an uncomfortable place may not necessarily be of the enemy. You may discover that it is God who is causing your pain, pushing you to the next level and into your destiny.

Think of a father who is teaching his daughter how to ride a bike. As long as he is running alongside of her, holding the seat straight, she tries very earnestly to ride the bike. After many tries, the father unbeknown to her, steps away from the bike and she rides on her own. But as soon as she notices that her father is no longer there, the girl panics and falls. With tearful eyes she looks back at her father, not understanding why he allowed her to fall. He waves to her from a distance and shows her how far she rode by herself. It wasn't until she doubted that she fell.

Similarly, if God doesn't push you, you would never launch into the deep. You would never move into all that God has for you. You will never know that you can ride by yourself.

Egyptian Bread

No doubt Joseph would have loved to stay with his father and brothers and not gone through all that he had. But there was a plan for Joseph's life. He was destined to go to Egypt to prepare the way for his brothers. God knew that thirteen years later, there would be a famine throughout the land (Gen. 42). God knew that He would have to keep the promise He made to Abraham, to bless his seed and cause them to prosper.

This example of Joseph teaches me that even if I don't understand the process, I have to trust the plan God has for my life. In the process He has made provision for me. In Egypt, there is bread. In the struggle, you will eat. In the suffering, you will not die. Right where you are, He is going to feed you. It may not be what you want to eat, but you will not go hungry. It may not be what you're used to wearing, but you won't be naked. Right in your Egypt, God has already made provision.

Nothing in Me

So then, what God teaches in the process becomes greater than the promise. In the process, pride is burned up and you learn that there is nothing in you worthy to receive anything from God. Therefore, when you reach your destiny and place of promise, you will give all glory to God. Before the process, you would have taken the credit. But after the process, you will confess that nothing in you was able to accomplish it.

Having experienced the oppression of suicidal thoughts and depression, I have become discerning of this spirit. I can sense when it is in the house. I can feel it on someone as I pass by. This is not so that I can act deep and spiritual. But because I have experienced it and know how it feels, I also know that God can deliver others from it.

Only God knows what is necessary to get us to the ultimate destination. He knows that there are some things in us that need to be dealt with now before we get to our final outcome. If He allows us to reach our destiny with the mess inside of us, we will not last. God knew that I needed to deal with areas of trust in order to survive the next dimension. God took me through a process that exposed everything that could not be used by Him.

Consider the potter who carefully and skillfully crafts a vessel into a beautiful work of art. To the layman, the vessel appears unblemished and ready to be set upon the highest shelf, but to the potter, the vessel's imperfection is glaring. He notices a flaw in the body of the vessel—a flaw that will not stand up against the heat of the kiln. So he remakes the vessel (Jer. 18.1-6).

God forms us after His will. He allows us to be tried in fire so that everything that is not like Him would be burned up. You thought it came to kill you; you thought you were going to die. But God sent it to make you better. God promises to prosper you, not to harm you (Jer. 29:11). He promised to finish what He started in you. He simply wants you to trust the plan.

The person who has always had a job and all his/her bills paid can only testify that God is the source if there is no longer a job and the way is still being made. The one who has been sick and is no longer can now testify that God is a healer. Only in times of torment and despair can God introduce Himself as Jehovah Shalom—God, our peace. How then will we know Him in all of His attributes if we do not come from behind our masks and let God be God?

Chapter 13
Take off the Mask

In this book I revealed myself to the world, and it was a liberating experience. Now, when things come to make me ashamed and uncomfortable, I examine the situation thoroughly and ask myself, "What is it that I am ashamed of? Who am I giving power over my life? Who is standing in judgment of me?"

1. Let Jesus cover you

I never used to pray to God about my feelings, fears, or failures. To the omniscient God I believed it was not necessary because He already knows everything. So I stifled my feelings and never expressed the sentiments of my heart. However, in this newfound liberty, I have realized that God loves relationship, and in relationship there is communication. If I were to sit in my room and cry, my husband—out of compassion—would naturally come to my side to find out what was troubling me. It would be unfair for me to tell him, "you know."

Even though he has loved me and lived with me for over thirteen years, he is not skilled in mind reading. He still needs me to articulate my needs. And when I do, he will try to appease me; he would go to the ends of the earth to satisfy my desire. Yet I would still be dissatisfied. I would still have a hunger and thirst that could not be quenched.

It is only Jesus who completely satisfies my longings. I could drink from the living fountain and never thirst again. I can eat from the living bread and never hunger. I don't have to wait for others to affirm me because the affirmation I need comes from the Father.

The Father who does not withhold any good thing from His children longs for us to sit and talk with Him. He wants to hear our concerns, failures, and fears. He wants us to confess our faults and weaknesses. He wants us to tell Him our dreams and goals. Our God desires relationship and wants to be involved with us during our failures and successes.

When this intimacy is in place, you will find that the Master will wrap His arm around you like no one else can. When you are insecure and fearful, allow Jesus to cover you with His loving arms. You will walk with a new rhythm in your step when you discover that you are not alone.

2. Write Your Feelings

Write in a journal. Someone once said that there is a book in all of us. The bookstores are full of life stories. Get a journal and write all of your fears. Begin with the shameful things you have done in your life. Examine your feelings. Are you still ashamed? Are you masking your feelings? Why are you hiding? Whom are you hiding from? Explore these feelings; be honest with yourself.

I have shared very personal things in this book. I am not necessarily asking you to do the same. This book started out as a journal, just a way for me to release feelings. You may be comfortable with just writing it down and when you have vented, you can destroy the pages. If you decide to keep it, put it in a safe place where no one will stumble upon it. I suggest that you also keep it out of your reach so that you won't be tempted to go back and rehash old feelings when you're having a bad day.

3. Allow Yourself to Heal

As you write it may be painful. You may uncover some feelings that you were not aware of. That is because we never allow ourselves to heal completely. Imagine having a sore and as soon as it begins to scab, you pick it until there is no more scab, so it causes you to bleed again. Similarly, when God is healing our wounds, often we don't allow Him to heal us completely. We start talking about how we got hurt, and we complain to anyone who would listen. What we are actually doing is pulling at the scab. Then, when we begin to bleed again, we run to our Father and show Him our "booboo."

My children Blair and Destiny are very close in age; they are often asked if they are twins. They have a close relationship and it is difficult for one to do something without the other. Blair can fall down, scrape his knee and run to me to clean his wounds. It would be my job to put him on my lap, cover it with bandage, and kiss his tears away. Destiny will soon follow, pointing at her knee, so that she could receive the same care. She's not hurt but simply wants the attention that comes with being wounded.

How many of us are wearing bandages but are really not wounded? We simply like the attention. We like people asking, "What happened to you?" We like people to pet us and kiss it and make it better. We are stuck in the healing process. However, in order to be made whole, you have to make the decision. When you really want to change, you will put away excuses. Then, with reckless abandonment, you will do whatever it takes to be whole.